The Art of the Sponge

The Art of the Sponge

A Handbook for Hosts and Houseguests

For Alison —
The best Hostess in Santa
Barbara — lessons for your
guests

Christina Griffin

Christina Griffin
2018

Illustrations by J. Marshall Smith

ISBN-13: 9781544173443
ISBN-10: 154417344X
Library of Congress Control Number: 2017903303
CreateSpace Independent Publishing Platform
North Charleston, South Carolina

Introduction

The act of Sponging, not to be confused with actually using a sponge in the cleanliness sense, is an ancient and universal art. It enjoys various titles—a "Parasite's Progress," the "Mooch March," and sundry other, probably less sanguine, nomenclature. But the idea is the same: to use one's friends, family, and, at last resort, business contacts, in order to rest for a fixed period of time in their lovely domiciles, be they in pricy urban areas or well-appointed vacation spots, so that one can stay for free and presumably also dine and drink "on the house" (pun intended!). It has been going on since Odysseus dropped in everywhere and William the Conqueror invited himself to England, and long may it flourish. After all, what is the point of having designer digs if one's intimates cannot enjoy them at leisure and marvel at how well the host lives? Or not.

That said, there are strict rules, unspoken and sometimes not understood, that must be followed if the visiting Sponger wishes to keep the host (the Spongee) on a receptive footing. Infractions (of course, even the most practiced Sponger has probably put a foot wrong occasionally) may result in a less-welcome mat the next time, or even in having the mat pulled altogether. So while the possibilities are infinite, the guidelines are exacting for maximum enjoyment of the visit.

While this modest guide is intended to enhance the pleasure of the Sponger, it also indicates necessary defensive maneuvers to the Spongee, should there be a particular objection to the prospective/descending guest/tribe. It is permissible to reject or make an excuse, but do so at your peril. Remember that Sponging is a two-way street, and the grapevine is strong and sinuous. So this book also offers profitable tips on how to be "best in show" so that friends and family will long want to toast—and taste—your hospitality!

———————

NB: This guide has been penned with the support of sundry members of Spongers USA and the approval of Spongers International (SI), President Emeritus the Hon. Benjamin Bowles, DHG, and his lovely lady Claire. All tactics herein have been analyzed and practiced, and every refinement has been considered. No bipeds were harmed in the testing of methods, and all ideas have every bearing on personal experience. No people, places, or things are coincidental.

The author, a well-known Sponger on both the national and international scene, has lived most of her life in Washington, a prime destination for visitors, as well as with her husband in India, Pakistan, Korea, Nigeria, Kenya, and Italy, some of which are more attractive to sponging houseguests than others. Her domestic experiences include most of the posh watering holes on the East Coast, New England, and Florida, as well as some delectable western and West Coast habitats, not including Los Angeles.

Chapter 1

Etiquette: Guest/Sponger

Before embarking on the finer points of Sponging, let me be clear that there are several cardinal rules of the game that must be firmly adhered to in order that the visit be a positive experience for both parties. These rules apply whether the impending mooch is domestic or international, unless of course it takes place in the Third World, in which case it all becomes subject to *force majeure* (French) or *forza maggiore* (Italian) or *what the hell* (English). All bets are off if you do not manage to get home in one piece.

For tamer horizons, however, please memorize the following (for best results):

- **Wheels**: Always arrive with your own. This will lull your host into thinking what a considerate guest you are, and he will be thrilled that he does not have to lug you around to futile visits to the airport for lost luggage, into town to buy the pills you forgot, or especially to go sightseeing, which he has done way too much of anyway. You are also subtly exhibiting your taste and style (BMW flash, VW eco-chic, minivan-prole). A car also provides you with a means of instant escape, should there erupt a flaming connubial row or a break in the hot-water heater.

- **Duration of Stay**: Optimum times can vary slightly depending on venue, but three nights (two to three days) suffice for most city respites; four nights (three to four days) the max for holiday houses. Not only will you probably run out of conversation on day three, after dissecting your mutual friends or bragging about your offspring, but you will actually be looking forward to not having to make polite conversation at all for a while.

  Corollary: Invent a valid reason for your departure so that your hostess can look genuinely sad as well as glad that she could not persuade you to stay on.

- **"Maid's Night Out" Meal**: Whether there is a servant or not, it is *de rigueur* that the Sponger take the Sponger (and spouse and offspring, if any) out for a meal at the Sponger's own expense. This can be tricky, as one must weigh the number of mouths to be fed versus how much of the host's "hospitality" has been consumed. Also, it depends on the availability of the "cheap and cheerful" option (if young mouths must be included) as opposed to the four-star *dinneria* that is "the only one around." Just grit your teeth, grip your wallet, and grin that you are dying to take everyone out in thanks for their generosity. Of course, if the hosts have been skimpy, then a lunch may fill the bill, as copious alcohol is usually not on the noontime agenda. Then again, maybe it is. Add to the fun by letting the host gingerly pull out his wallet as the bill arrives before you grandly wave him away with a flash of your Amex Platinum!

Chapter 2

Etiquette: Host/Spongee

With the pleasurable anticipation of having guests come to stay, the Spongee should plan to ensure the comfort of her arriving

- single/divorced old friend / distant cousin / college roommate (pick one);
- great couple from a distant venue, school chums of any persuasion, closest/farthest relative, and new mate (pick some); or
- horde of hellish in-laws with bored teenage children or ex-neighbors who believed it when told, "Come see us!" (optimum pick: none).

Never mind. Live there, and they will come.

All guests with a modicum of sense know that when it comes to vacation houses or yachts, it is best to let one's friends do the actual owning. The host has the dubious pleasure of the building and maintenance costs, allowing his guests unfettered free stays. But the benefits to the hostess cannot be overemphasized.

First, delightful hosts, you are the owner of a

- **house/apartment** in a city of some note, about which you and your mate have spent hours of arguing on the color of the walls or where to hang the grandparents (preferably yours and not bought at auction). The kitchen has cost a fortune, and the decorator bills have almost been paid.

Or a

- **country house**, either in the hills or at the beach, preferably at or near a famous watering hole, where authentic "shabby chic" reigns in the third-generation family manse (or *faux* shabby if new). Ideally, the china should have a few chips, and the towels should never match, but no guest will complain if you bought new, as long as the beds are comfortable and the bathroom works.

Or a

- **yacht,** of which you are justly proud, because we all know the old saw that if you own it, it must cost a fortune, and if one has to ask, one cannot afford it, etc. Boats are a special niche-spongedom, as only a few special people want to be tossed around on the seas and get their hair all messy and throw up in their cabins and so forth.

NB: In this age of traveling gadgets, it is practically *de rigueur* to provide Wi-Fi and power strips for your visitors. No amount of picturesque rusticity will make up for a lack of electronic connectivity. In fact, it may cause guests to resort to early departures.

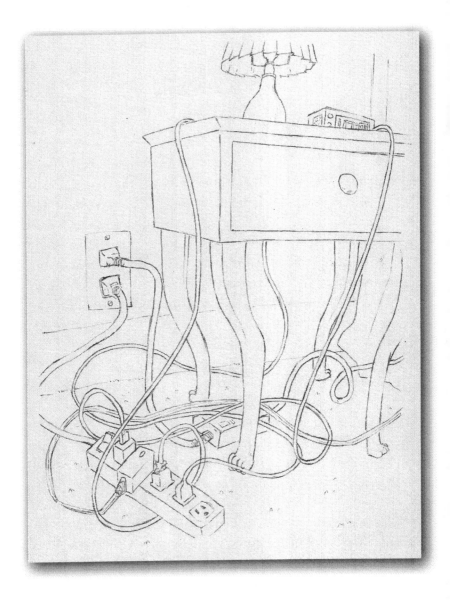

Your newly arrived guests will do the obligatory "oohs" and "aahs" when they enter your domicile, remarking on the taste and comfort that you are providing them for the next several days. A great view of a golf course, a mountain, or the sea is always a huge plus, but barring that, the knowledge that yours is an area worthy of place-dropping will provide the proper amount of *cachet* to float your reputation among the sponging *cognoscenti* as a refuge of style.

Secondly, and perhaps of more immediate use, is that Spongers provide you an excuse to entertain all those people you owe but who prove difficult to include in more intimate (i.e., among close friends) occasions. The dread of several evenings alone with your guests will spur an inspired and enthusiastic invitation to acquaintances that you might otherwise find too (a) controversial, (b) stuffy, or (c) tiresome to come for dinner/lunch with "our guests" from Rome, Nairobi, or Cleveland. Not only will you impress your houseguests with your largesse, but you will also finesse a group of "duty diners" in one fell swoop—be sure to invite as many as possible to get them all over with at once. Plus, numbers dilute the above obvious flaws. A win-win all around!

NB: It is advisable with such above one-off meals to invest in proper food and drink (as opposed to plonk wine you might serve to close friends). The hostess should either make an effort to cook a real meal or, barring any culinary talent, find the nearest caterer/deli to provide nourishment so that all the guests (local and imported) feel they have been feted. Of course, should they descend a second time, they should be treated like anyone else!

Chapter 3

The Setup

*T*ruly practiced Spongers *announce* their arrival. Neophytes should probably request.

Whether a summer vacation, winter break, spring folly, or fall getaway—there are so many possibilities to find friends who need and deserve to have you come for a visit! Be imaginative!

The season, reason, destination, and length of visit should be determined well in advance, if for no other reason than to give your target host fewer excuses to deny you.

Lord Bowles, Founder of Spongers International (mentioned in the introduction), sent the following message to a potential target in Tuscany: "I propose that Claire and I come see you whilst our mutual friends are with you. We can get a cheap flight from Bristol to Pisa that morning. Would it also be possible for you to meet us there, or should we struggle by coach to Siena?"

His covering explanation was this: "The real art of being a world-class Sponger is to make it impossible for the targeted 'Spongee' to actually say NO *to the Sponger-in-Waiting. Don't you agree? I think my e-mail has sufficient charms, guile, and subtle undertones of the arse-licking genre to make it impossible for him to turn down my offer of five days of high-end sponging, as well as the potentially huge inconvenience of coming to meet us at the airport!"*

———————

There is the **single sponge**, such as the theatre night in New York, the 60th birthday party in London, or the friend's destination wedding in Sonoma Valley. These events usually are mercifully short and require no payback, at least in the short term. For any such event, comb your Rolodex (oh, how quaint—I mean your contact list) for friends (depending on exigency, acquaintances may suffice *in extremis*) in the focus area.

A variation on the above is the slightly more self-centered **sport sponge**, intending only that you wish to avail yourself of your host's tennis club (or better, his private court); ditto of his membership at a seriously swish local golf course—Augusta, Piping Rock, *et alia*—after which you can brag/place-drop *ad nauseam* to your less fortunate friends.

That you might have lobbied your host for an invitation to play in an exclusive tournament should barely be mentioned. The golf Sponger should insist on paying the guest fee and caddy expenses. Determine the caddy fee with your host at the 17th green, and present the caddy with his tip in plain sight—but folded in half, of course.

And you tennis people, attention! Always assume that white is the operative *dictat*. Ladies, never, *ever* show up assuming that you may look like Serena in full plumage, no matter your skills. And gentlemen, only ever wear collared shirts. T-shirts are taboo on a court (and should be everywhere), and you do not wish to look as if you left home in your underwear.

Next, decide if the trip could/should be turned into a **serial sponge**, if time permits. Not surprisingly, the serial involves finding multiple targets in the same general geography (viz., New England, Florida, anywhere in Italy), on whom one can count to find a bed for a night, or preferably several (see introduction). This is a more complicated trip and therefore may necessitate being flexible in deference to the target host's other engagements—make sure that he or his dwelling will be available for your visit. The **serial** can be combined with the **sport** but involves way more date arrangement.

A friend tells of the archetypal winter ski getaway, which involved contacting old boarding-school pals and ex–business chums with second chalets in such coveted ski areas as Sun Valley, Jackson Hole, Aspen, Vail, and Squaw Valley. A lot of hard planning time had been needed to make sure all would be suitably ensconced at the proper time (midwinter); but according to plan, he strung together multiple hosts to ski glamorously for six weeks straight with nary a hotel bill or meal ticket in sight!

The *ne plus ultra* is the **absent-host sponge**, where one is invited to stay alone in the London flat, the Provençal *maison*, or the Chesapeake estate for the week; the key is under the mat, and there is wine in the fridge. Be my guest! Now you have hit the jackpot! The considerate host will not only contrive to be away for a good long stretch and provide you with a written list of house-y quirks and pitfalls, but he will also not burden you with any pets.* A car thrown in is a sure rocket to the A-list—a very rare event, but it can happen.

*A near tragedy was averted years ago, when my not-quite-husband and I were staying at the penthouse suite of Canadian diplomat / soon-to-be-parents friends in New York. We would cat-sit (and cockatoo-sit) for the Labor Day weekend.

The cat had recently lost her mate, who had fallen from the upper-floor terrace balcony, so our hosts had brought in a kitten to keep the distraught widow cat company.

I am allergic to cats.

The mother cat decided that my bed was where she wanted to suckle kitten. I came in from sunbathing on the terrace and tried to remove her from the bed.

N-q-h then heard shrieks and found me standing on the back of the living-room sofa, streaming blood from cat claws all over my bikini-clad body.

He threw me in the shower.

He threw the cats into another bathroom. Widow/mother cat yowled a lot.

For the next three days, cat, when allowed out, stalked me like a tiger if I opened my mouth.

The hosts returned on Monday night and did not believe our tale. When I came out to greet them, cat, who had been sneaking around on the back of the sofa, flew in full attack mode at me through the air, claws and teeth out. N-q-h caught cat midair, to the astonishment of hosts.

Subsequently, as only can happen in New York, cat went to a pet psychiatrist...the pregnant wife had her baby...the husband left the wife for the au pair.

———

Once the target trip has been decided, it is time to consider...

Chapter 4

What to Bring

Equipment

The roof rack is a marvelous invention: versatile, for skis for the visit to chalet chums in the Rockies; commodious, for those extra suitcases, or even better, the "Clam," which can hold a host of sports gear such as golf clubs, tennis racquets, and presumably even surfboards.

Cousin to the roof rack, the rear-end bicycle rack looks positively ominous when loaded with a full complement of wheels. A fully loaded minivan with all the above, plus a gang of passengers, can inspire awe on the highway and a frisson of foreboding in the Spongee who watches it arrive in her driveway—as in, "How long are these people planning to stay anyway?"

Always assure your hostess with a deprecatory laugh that you just "want to be ready for anything" planned, so there is no need to borrow. She will probably have you park this mobile monster behind the house in any case, so it cannot be construed by uppity neighbors as a commercial vendor—or worse, noisy interlopers—parked in the front yard.

Luggage

The temptation to bring far too many clothes is strong, especially for those who were born in the era of sea travel and porters. Alas,

those days are a memory, so today's guests should curb their enthusiasm for steamer trunks and the equivalent and whittle down to one or two wheelies that will not give the helpful host a hernia as he leads you to the third-floor guest room.

Packing in lots of bags from Trader Joe's or Tiffany's is also frowned upon, as no matter the implied name-dropping, paper-packing exudes an aura of disorganized peasantry.

My dear husband is of the old school of sailing/steamer trunks and porters. It has taken me a lifetime to wean him away from large 60+-lb. suitcases to two 30-lb. versions ("You never know what we'll need"). Inevitably, the taller the house, the heavier the cases. To be fair, these overweight problems have often involved moving residence from, say, Karachi to Washington; but on several occasions, I have watched our hostess go ashen at the sight of such a luggage array, and arrangements have had to be made to store stuff in a lower-level potty or the like.

And it is such fun to repack in the middle of an airport!

It is a long and unwinnable battle, I fear.

Useful tip: If traveling by road, throw all the clothes you might possibly want in a large, see-through plastic box in the trunk. Then, put a few things in a dainty overnight bag. If you find you need new, clean, or different duds, you can sneak out to your car when no one is around, and presto, a whole new wardrobe!

Clothing

In an earlier era, the watchwords for ladies were *evening dress* and *bathing suit*—if one showed up with these items of apparel in private houses or chic watering holes, one was totally safe, presuming one brought other clothes also. Ditto for gentlemen: *black tie (tuxedo)* and swimsuit. In today's world, alas, the casual has taken over, and even well-heeled people dress like peons, in floppy T-shirts, baggy pants, and flip-flops—even on airplanes! Never mind; we will not enter into this sartorial quagmire here. But the above advice is still applicable: just substitute *black pants* for evening dress and a *blazer* and *tie* for the dinner jacket. It is almost inconceivable that, no matter the season, these fashion items will not be needed. Even if your hostess says that all will be *blue jeans*, do not believe it for a moment.

Or do, but s*nappy* jeans with *proper* jewelry and *good* shoes will never be out of place.

Well, OK, maybe in the wilds of Alaska or the Kenyan bush, they might be, but it is a good "uniform" (with a top added) for visits to urban civilization.

NB: Special to ladies—shoes make or break an outfit; that cannot be overstated. Ergo, good shoes are a must, even if your clothes are lackluster. Your feet will pave the way! Complement your *ensemble* with proper jewelry—real, if possible. In recent times, accessories in plastic, felt, or tire rubber have gained popularity in a sort of we-the-people way, but never underestimate the *cachet* of gold—or silver, if you swing that way.

Chapter 5

Children? Or Dogs?

How well you know your prospective host will determine the vital answers to many questions that will necessarily come up. Surprise is probably not a good option in this area.

Children

Of course, it would have been more considerate of you not to own any rug rats or teenagers to begin with, but since you do, you must make the concept of a visiting horde appear attractive to the host.

Please try to instill in your offspring that in someone else's house, it is not kosher to dive into the refrigerator, hurl themselves on the sofa and turn on the TV, or talk on their cell phones during a meal.

Ditto the littler ones, even grandchildren, who should at least be housebroken.

If the host has corresponding darlings, then life becomes simpler, and one hopes that all kids can be quarantined in a large, fully equipped basement and left there indefinitely—or go out to chaperoned affairs elsewhere, where the other parents are in charge.

Dog

Pets can be a touchy subject, in that there exist people who do *not do* animals—unimaginable, I know you will agree, but there you are. Still, most normal people will welcome your dog (less so, your cat) as a conversation piece or surrogate child.

Personally, I have always thought that dogs are better behaved than most people's children, as they don't argue and pout and are always pleasant to be around. A small dog is more portable and convenient than the big guy with the coffee-table tail, but as long as the dog does not eat small children, any size should be welcome.

Dogs, plural, should probably be avoided, as they might embark on a barking marathon, not to mention a feeding and pooping frenzy. It goes without saying that your dog should also be house-broken, continent, and preferably trained to do a trick or two.

Over the years, the author has traveled with three dogs—consecutively—who I know have brought joy to all they visited.

*   ***Willie*** *was a superlative, patrician dachshund who, being "unfixed," took off in each new Sponge neighborhood, often entailing long runs of everyone in the house in pursuit, calling for him. One hostess did have the good grace to say how Willie's escape inspired "camaraderie" among her dinner guests!*

*   ***Buddy****, a controllable but rather dopey dax (never say "wiener dog"), was transfixed by flashing lights, mirrors, and dancing shadows (as in laundry on a line), and could be amused for hours by a flashlight. That last quirk could render him quite noisy if you were looking for a nocturnal bathroom with a light in a strange house.*

*   ***Rollo****, a sort-of dax, has just returned from his first serial Sponge this summer, where he had delighted all (not) with his eager dash to every human-seating surface. His one trick, sitting up on his hind legs and being unbearably cute, has ensured possible return visits.*

Chapter 6

Health

Allergies

Allergies can prove a plus or a minus, depending on their type. They prove very useful should you find yourself facing a certain food that you detest: "Sorry, but I am allergic to peanut stew" (black-eyed peas, organ meats, kale, or other exotic fare) can be your watchword! Or "I get asthma when I climb mountains" will get you out of that dreary two-mile trudge in the rain.

It is quite unacceptable, however, to necessitate a trip to the emergency room because of tripping off a front step or falling into the bushes, for whatever alcoholic reason. If you should encounter overlooked dust or mold in the guestroom, hang your head out the window, and put all your antihistamines to work!

Finally, always blame your hangover on the "sulfites" in the wine; it sounds very chemical and arcane and casts doubt on the quality of the libations of the night before—ergo, not your fault!

An exception to the hospital visit, however, occurs when the Dog of the House decides that you are the Enemy for no particular reason, and your arm becomes a tasty hors d'oeuvre. This type of event almost always happens on a weekend night, making the dash to the medico all the more fraught as you dodge the drunks and the accident-prone in the waiting room. The injured guest should probably not dwell on the pain and suffering incurred, but may enjoy a little added vengeance in causing a guilt trip for the hostess, lest anyone forget!

Dietary Needs

Barring the above allergies, you must not expect your hostess to welcome whatever food fetishes you may be presently practicing. Do not stuff the refrigerator with your tofu, soy milk, yeast extract, or rabies serum to the displacement of the hostess's designer, farm-fresh food, bought at great expense for you.

Conversely, if the host fridge is already stuffed with the above exotic food groups, then it is acceptable to suggest that you go out and buy normal foods, such as eggs or cheese or ice cream—at your expense, naturally—so that you can tactfully indicate that you will starve to death otherwise.

This is also a good time to volunteer to cook a dinner, with the compliance of other guests, so that you can be assured of at least one good meal, should the converse seem even a remote threat. (See "The House Present.")

Friends' experiences on this subject fall into the following range:

- The excessively generous host, who not only offers his liquor-cabinet and wine-cellar contents without bounds but also the labors of his designer-cooking wife, who adores presenting homemade meals nonstop. (Italian)
- The parsimonious hostess, who provides guests with the minimal breakfast supplies (bread, cereal, milk) and actively encourages all the house-party participants to

bring cases of wine, liquor, and different food menus. This one can also be notoriously absent when it comes time to pay at the supermarket. (American)

- And everyone in between.

———

Teetotalers—what to say? Should you be bent in that direction, have the grace not to ignore the fun and hilarity of fellow guests, but nurse your beverage of choice in bemused silence. (Others will assume you are on the wagon "for a reason," and they should quickly recover from their surprise/pity.) Conversely, you should be allowed a pass to retire at a reasonable time, before the "lamp-shades-on-head" hour.

Chapter 7

The House Present

*I*ronically, the choice of a house present is one of the more difficult aspects of any prospective visit and has caused many Spongers-in-waiting long moments of brain- wracking and hair-pulling. It is essential to get it approximately right, as it reflects on your taste as the guest, as well as on your perception of the recipient.

The present is *de rigueur*, so ignore at your peril, lest you be considered boorish or, worse, cheap. This applies to close friends, mere acquaintances, and *especially* family members (relatives are not exempt just because of presumed entitlement).

Mainly, the gift should be presented with the sincerest gratitude, no matter if unforeseen issues, such as political discussions or marital feuds, occurred during the stay.

An after-present is also acceptable, if a guest should arrive empty-handed. For full credit, make sure that the host is aware that a memorable picture album or a designer food package is imminent.

Usual Gift Choices

Comestibles are the safest, as one always need food and drink, and more mature hosts usually want/require no more "things" (unless it is a grandchild's first pottery effort or a similar bibelot).

- Wine: good to acceptable quality—or at least recognizable
- Designer chocolates: ditto, but never Ferrero Rocher
- Buying and cooking a meal while in residence is always happily received

Books, especially the coffee-table variety, are another showy offering of which we probably all have too many. Do, however, align the book to the Spongee—nothing reeks of secondhand-edness more than an ill-matched *Fishing in Patagonia* presented to a computer geek (even if he owns the company) or *Mosaics of Ravenna* to the Bergdorf shopaholic. Used cookbooks will always give themselves away. [See Regifting, below].

Otherwise, consider

- an oeuvre of "gravitas" and/or importance;
- a (signed) memoir (extra points);
- the latest bestseller, but above the caliber of James Patterson; or
- a dishy *roman à clef*, as long as it does not relate to the family of the host

Household Bric-a-Brac

- Generic platters, vases, glasses (always well received, again of good quality or at least in expensive wrapping);
- Monogrammed anything: "his" and "her" matching?— maybe, maybe not;
- NB: *Nothing* that looks like a recycled wedding present or shower gift

Unusual Gift Choices

- Homemade items: your signed artwork, a hand-carved walking stick, a repurposed flower pot, and so on (with discretion);
- Items from Victoria's Secret (iffy)
- A drone (A+ for originality)
- A copy of this book (A+ for taste)

Other Considerations

NB: **Regifting** is a subject of much debate. Is it acceptable—isn't it always? But carefully. We all harbor a drawer or closet full of beautiful soaps, guest towels, and the like, much of which we know would look so much better in someone else's house.

Heirlooms are always good to palm off on younger family members, especially if they are graduating, getting married, or celebrating just about anything. Polish that silver *bonbonnière* or serving dish from your grandmother and bestow it with solemnity on the anointed ones. They will gush thanks and promptly stick it in a drawer forever. (Most of the young these days do not want real anything, which is why auction houses are full up with unsold family silver.)

Foreign items—picked up with such enthusiasm on a trip and viewed with such contempt when reaching home—are obvious regifting choices. But that tribal mask, that hand-woven sisal pointy thing, or those prayer beads may not be as exotic and desirable as you once thought and will completely mystify your hosts.

Finally, and if you pay attention to nothing else, *never* make a gift of **scented candles!** They are completely out of the question. Donate them to Goodwill.

Chapter 8

International Sponging

This subject has been touched upon above, but herewith are a few observations of personal experience.

Foreigners are very different from thee and me. They operate under different sets of rules, depending on background and country of origin.

The **British**, as is well known, are the past masters of the Sponge, probably having invented it. They are known for staying for days, weeks, or even months. This is probably the result of the Empire, wherein once one got to another corner of same, one could not be expected to leave in a hurry. For the most part, they will amuse and charm you and your other guests, and they speak in their delicious accent that Americans find pure catnip.

They are also wizards at parking their children on you for the duration, as in, "Hermione is doing an internship for her gap year—would you look out for her?"

An English lady I know invited her daughter to stay with an American friend in Kenya "for a bit." Four weeks later the girl had not only stayed, eaten, laundered clothes, and taken over the guest-room, but she also had managed to decamp to another friend for a week or so. A sponge-begetting sponge! She must have finally left, but there was never a thank-you note to prove it.

Continental Europeans in general need slightly more pampering and should not be encouraged unless they come with benefits, as in a *schloss, chateau,* or *villa.* The men especially need tending, as they expect to have their slightest whim catered to, have food produced seamlessly as at home, and have the room made up daily. And bemoan the sartorial standards of well-heeled Europeans, as they exude an elegance that can put the average American host into depression.

It rarely occurs to the European guest that happily consumed food or drink could be replenished.

The Greeks, an urbane friend points out, have a term for the undesirable stay: the "Armenian visit," whereby the guests arrive on very short notice, bring no gift, overstay their time, and were not particularly welcome to begin with.

The flip side, of course, is to return the favor abroad and to take your gentle revenge by enjoying their hospitality at length, at the aforementioned *schloss, chateau,* or *villa.*

It is often even more difficult to entertain **South Americans,** who swoop in and do everything with a larger-than-life flair that can sometimes be overwhelming to us more buttoned-up neighbors to the north. It is probably easier to visit them than to contemplate trying to live up to their over-the-top hospitality standards of plenteous food and drink, wonderful music, and spectacular domiciles. One visitor tells of a beautiful free apartment overlooking the Rio Bay, a private yacht trip organized just for him and his wife, and a weekend visit to a private mountain palace, all within the first week.

You just have to relax and enjoy it all, against your Puritan instincts.

Asians are very polite and can be most unobtrusive and charming Spongers—until it comes to your kitchen, which they will invade with their culinary challenges and take over with exotic diets and cooking implements. This is not necessarily a bad thing, except that you will never get the aroma of curry or *kimchi* out of your curtains. Invite with discretion.

NB: All of the above Sponger rules shall still apply.

Visiting in **Africa** needs a special paragraph, as your hosts there are delighted to receive guests from the First World and even from the Second. They are extremely generous with their hospitality, food, and drink and seem eager for you to stay on indefinitely. This may have something to do with having hot- and cold-running servants, so that meals, laundry, and flowers appear as if by magic. With the Internet and the cell phone, they rarely see the need to come see you.

A word to the wise: Always keep a good friend in London (or other default target city) who will reliably have you to stay, as the best international cities are now prohibitively expensive (even in Australia), and your mood will be dampened by paying too much for lodging. The reciprocal meal (see above) will be bad enough!

Chapter 9

Yeas and Nays (for Guests)

If, after all that you have learned thus far, you *still* need to be told a few basic behavioral hints to insure your continued welcome, then herewith a few quirky thoughts.

Do...

- Be enthusiastic about helping out with household chores, such as washing up after meals, slicing and dicing, taking out trash, and so forth. Offer to remake beds as you leave, although that onus can be avoided by having to catch a plane or some such.
- Make an effort to talk to all pleasantly, even if the conversation bores you to tears. There is usually someone in any group who has to tell you more than you ever need to know about any given subject. Try not to let your eyes glaze over—hopefully, there will be a newspaper around. And telling jokes at breakfast should be strictly avoided.
- Pat the dog(s), even if you don't *do* dogs.
- Should you have depleted the hostess's store of premium vodka or a favorite pâté, be couth enough to offer to replace it. People have been known to get cranky when the cupboard is bare.

- Should a domestic/marital feud erupt, which happens more than one would expect, either (p.m.) dive into your guest bedroom and shut the door immediately, or (a.m.) wheel off quickly to sightsee, shop, or find the nearest bar. Stay away five hours.

Do not...

- Assume a servant (should one even exist) is there to do your laundry or ironing, or baby-sit your offspring or dog (unless approved by your hostess). If so, a generous *pourboire* is expected. Time to grin at your wallet.
- Arise too early to jog, say, as it may set off the alarm or wake the dogs. Ditto getting up too late to miss what passes for breakfast, as preset foods have a short life visually, and the hostess is already worrying about lunch.
- Use up all the hot water, especially in rustic retreats—it might be the week's supply.

And never...

- Plug up toilets with a massive use of toilet paper (you know who you are).
- Expect your host to retrieve/return lost luggage or other detritus that you have left under the bed.
- *Ever* do the Sunday crossword puzzle—or the Sudoku—without the express consent of the hostess. This transgression alone may cause major frostiness or result in death.

Chapter 10

Pulling the Rug (for Hosts)

There are times, dear Sponger, when even the most generous or gullible hosts will finally lose their collective rag and decide that they have had enough of feeding and watering the multitudes. This should in no way be taken as an insult—unless for some reason you have brought this on yourself, such as with an incontinent child or dog or a massive breach of etiquette on your part (see previous chapter). There are just times when the desire to protect the hosts' privacy must be respected, and you must fall back on Plan B (i.e., another Sponge target).

Various excuses are available to hosts who wish to discourage—or dread—any more guests. Random variations are offered below for foolproof protection, though beware the buzz that may ensue should any of these reasons need to be verified!

- Infestation of bedbugs in the guestroom (does not reflect well on your housekeeping, but you can blame previous guests)
- X (husband, child, dog, maid) undergoing some incapacitating health issue, such as rehab, a nervous breakdown, or chemo, among others (with extreme caution, lest a massive condolence drive ensue on Twitter)

- Asbestos, mold, radon, (other) gas leaks discovered (or one of the latest litigious *über*problems per the local real estate agent)
- House being used as a filming location for a TV series for an unknown length of time (risky if friends still watch TV—be vague)
- Totally full up with visiting family, godchildren, old roommates, ex-lovers, new lovers, and so forth, for the foreseeable future (safest)
- The option of complete honesty—"ve vant to be alone"—sometimes the most difficult for your Sponging friends to digest

Finally, here's the ultimate way to put off the moochers: be crazy. This delightful letter appeared in a British magazine recently and read in part,

"Mr. X of Bath has my complete respect revealing that he was able to get rid of unwanted guests by his wife running round naked in the garden. I have been searching for this type of service for ages. Do you think she might assist at a party we are planning in the Fall?"

End

Notes

Notes

Notes

Notes

Notes

Notes

Notes

Notes

Notes

Notes

Made in the USA
Columbia, SC
18 December 2017